Advance Praise for *TreeTalk*

That these poems started out as leaves can be felt in the reading. There is a vitality to this work that is verdant. The poems read as if they are still outside, golden-houred. Ariel Gordon has curated a space for herself and for her community in the company of an elm. And we are the fortunate recipients of a collection to share, to read aloud, for the tree of it. — **Sue Goyette**

Ariel Gordon, truly the Jane Jacobs of trees and poetry, has charmed a multitude of strangers and passersby to sing small songs to the urban canopy, to whisper their secrets and confessions to a neighbourhood elm tree. The result is *TreeTalk*, a celebration of the city-dweller's relationship with trees, but also an elegy to the stress and devastation imposed on urban nature in the course of "growing" and developing a city. In *TreeTalk*, Ariel Gordon not only re-foliates a tree with poems, she adds a startling and crucial layer of leaves to how we might (re)imagine ourselves coexisting with nature.
— **Sylvia Legris**

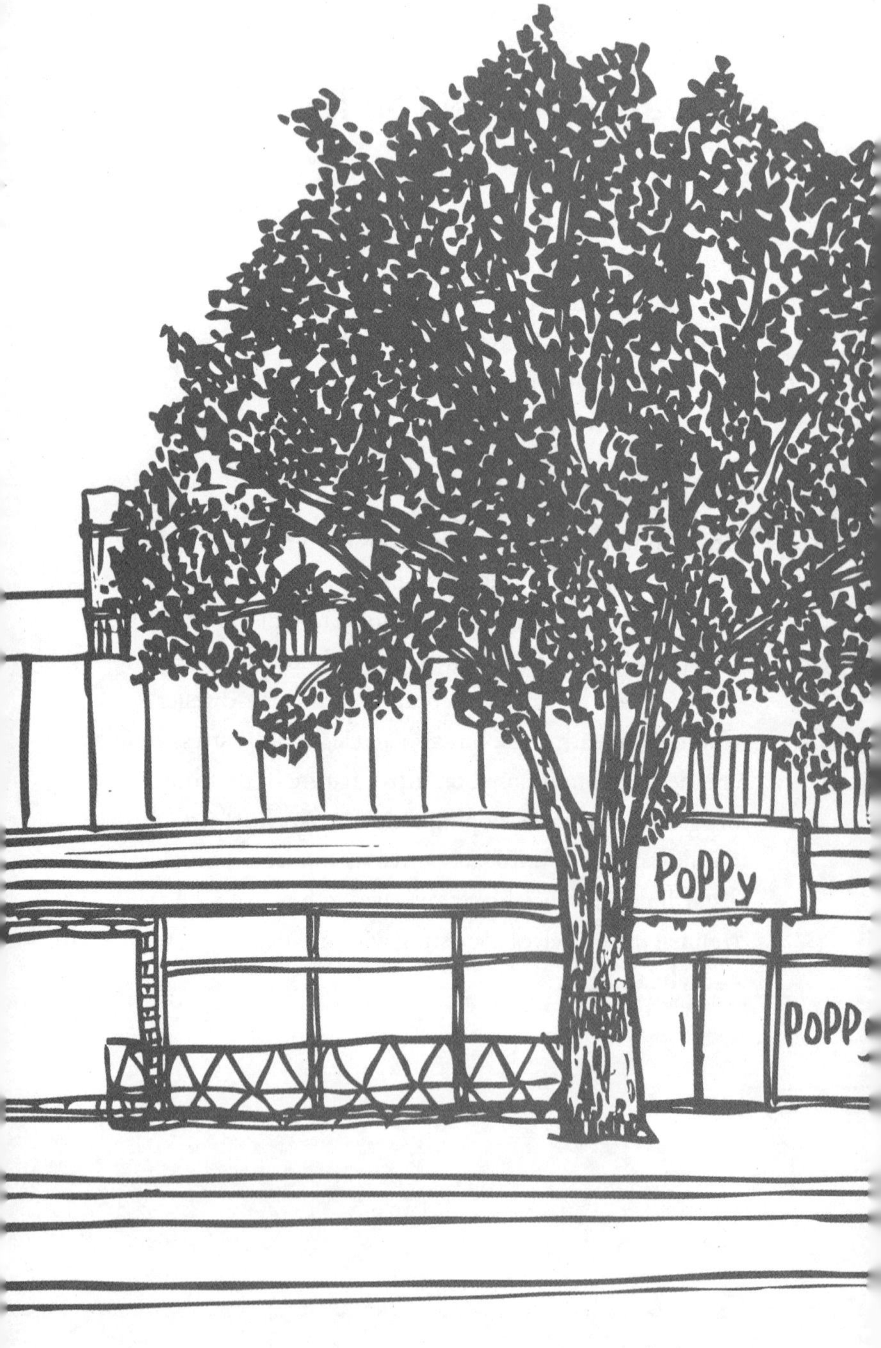

PoPPy
POPP

TreeTalk

TreeTalk

Ariel Gordon
With illustrations by Natalie Baird

WINNIPEG

TreeTalk

Copyright © 2020 Ariel Gordon
Illustrations copyright © 2020 Natalie Baird

Design by M. C. Joudrey and Matthew Stevens.
Layout by Matthew Stevens and M. C. Joudrey.

Published by At Bay Press September 2020.

All rights reserved. The use of any part of this publication, reproduced, transmitted in any form or by any means electronic, mechanical, photocopying, recording or otherwise, or stored in a retrieval system without prior written consent of the publisher or in the case of photocopying or other reprographic copying, license from the Canadian Copyright Licensing Agency-is an infringement of the copyright law.

No portion of this work may be reproduced without express written permission from At Bay Press.

Library and Archives Canada cataloguing in publication is available upon request.

ISBN 978-1-988168-27-2

Printed and bound in Canada.

This book is printed on acid free paper that is 100% recycled ancient forest friendly (100% post-consumer recycled).

First Edition

10 9 8 7 6 5 4 3 2 1

atbaypress.com

Introduction

On July 29-30, 2017, I sat on The Tallest Poppy's patio as part of a Synonym Art Consultation residency, looking up into the boulevard elm and writing snippets of poems, which I hung from the boulevard tree using paper and string. Passersby were invited to TreeTalk, too — their secrets / one-liners / meditations / haikus were also hung from the tree.

By the end of the weekend, the elm had a second, temporary canopy of leaves: 234 poems—111 written by me, 107 written by passersby and 16 from other sources.

Four more TreeTalk books will follow this one, written as part of Saskatchewan's Sage Hill Writing Experience in 2019, the Winnipeg Folk Festival's 2019 Prairie Outdoor Exhibition, and the Prairie Gate Literary Festival at the University of Minnesota, Morris during a catastrophic snowstorm that destroyed thousands of trees on public and private property.

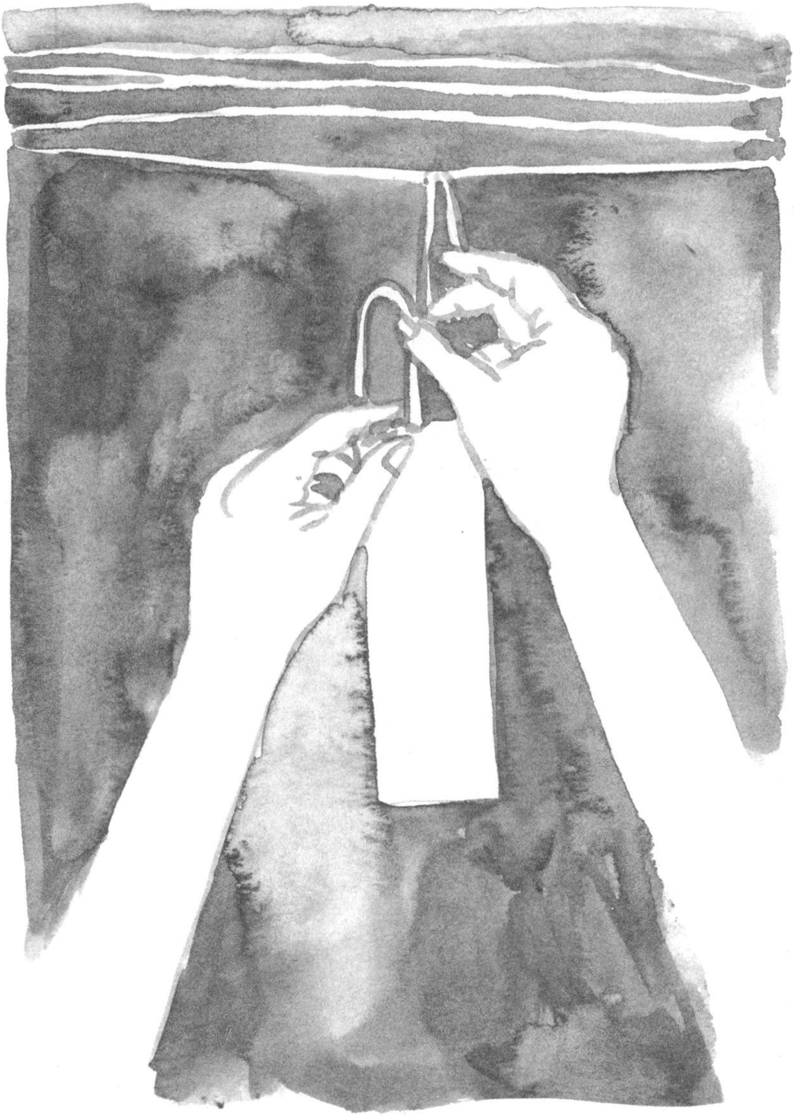

Ariel Gordon

American Elm. Also known as White, River, Water or Soft Elm. *Ulmus americana.*

Sat., 7/29, Hi/Lo: 29°C /20°C

The horizon filled with crosses, strings of lights, doors & windows. A dead elm down the street from this tree, this perch. Telling time by the bus schedule,

the number of yolks broken

in the breakfast rush.

TreeTalk

"The graceful, spreading crown of American Elm makes this one of our most easily recognized trees." — *Plants of the Western Boreal Forest & Aspen Parkland*

How do you talk to a tree?
With sentences as broad as a year? Sudden storms of words.
Squirrels as punctuation.

Old women with wheeled carts. Young women with iced coffees. Men with windows rolled down. The clink of ice in a glass. A motorcycle idling at the red light, his slow arc into traffic.

Ariel Gordon

A young Indigenous man is the first to approach.
He circles the patio. Finally, he sits & stares
at the tree. *Spell thanks,* he says
& waits. *Spell mother. Spell earth.*

TreeTalk

"Dutch elm disease [DED], caused by the wilt fungus (*Ceratocystis ulmi*) and spread by elm bark beetles, was introduced accidentally to North America around 1930, and was first recorded in Manitoba in 1975. Since then, many trees have died." — *Plants of the Western Boreal Forest*

The place where the bulldozer backed into it. The place where a chainsaw bit, clumsily…

Poems are made by losers like me,
But only the city can plant a boulevard tree.

Ariel Gordon

Virgo Supercluster
Milky Way
Orion Arm
Solar System
Earth
North America
Canada
Manitoba
Winnipeg
Wolseley
103 Sherbrook Street

TreeTalk

Most Cellphones Unlocked.
Wasps patrolling the middle distance.
We Buy GOLD. A truck honking across the street.

> "The burning issues of today are the ashes of tomorrow, but a noble elm is a verity that does not change with time." — *Donald Culross Peattie, A Natural History of North American Trees*

People approach. People circle, checking things out.
They sit & stare at the tree, their pens hovering over the paper. CONFESS!

Ariel Gordon

I help people tie their snippets to the tree.

The leaves sway above & below. The tree doesn't move.

So many bare branches.

Such a full canopy.

TreeTalk

Dear Tree: Thanks for the shade, the leaves, and for keeping watch on us all in our frailty, industry, doubt + glory.

I like to think about the things you must have seen…

A pennywhistle in a panhandler's beard. A gleaming marigold in a boulevard planter. Shouting.

Elms & haze. The tip of a cane,

striking the ground.

Ariel Gordon

The invisibility of trees. Battered furniture, set out
on the curb like it was moving day. Stout pipe no one
notices until it bursts.

> Thank you for giving us clean air. I'm sorry for
> what we are doing to you. I want us to be better.

I am shaded, cooled.

I am canopied, in good

company. I am treed.

Ariel Gordon

> "One of our finest shade trees, widely used as an ornamental tree in cities and rural areas across much of Canada." — *Plants of the Western Boreal Forest*

This poem can be summed up in three words:
paper + string + tree.

A bus huffs, hunched over its wheels.
A duo of white woman
wait, moving in
& out of the dappled light.

> "What can you use elm wood for? Do elm trees grow fast? Is elm wood a hard wood? Where does the elm tree grow?" — *People Also Ask, Google.com*

TreeTalk

This tree filters gleam. This tree a sun-lover,
a sweetie-pie,
a mouth-breather.

>Dear Tree, may you bring peace to this
>neighbourhood…

Ariel Gordon

Sundresses. Shredded fishnet stockings.
Hawaiian shirts. Cut-off shorts & slashed band T-shirts.
Aprons & ear buds.

How do you contain a tree?
I can't reach all the way around, but I've tanglefooted
a few lines to your trunk. I've belted you.

TreeTalk

CONFESSION: I once spent a sweet hour cutting an entire tree into firewood, an hour perfecting my swing. The tree split, it knotted. Sawdust flew. And all of it was fed to the fire, turning my skin smoky.

SECRET: I don't think having murderous thoughts is a bad thing.

Ariel Gordon

The breeze redeems the street. The shadows deepen.
I can't get over people reaching up to refoliate the tree.
People bending & thinking *tree*, instead of *morning,
cream for my tea…*

TreeTalk

Leaves & paper. Wasps' nests. Manuscripts. Parasols. Cones & flowers & seeds. Napkins on the ground.

> "Elms produce massive amounts of seed that can soon cover the ground with seedlings. This can be a problem when trees close to houses fill eavestroughs with their fruits." — *Plants of the Western Boreal Forest*

Ariel Gordon

The wind musses the leaves, pushes my hair
into the corners of my eyes.
The clouds are stacked high. Traffic dense
& then, the street EMPTY.

SECRET: I fear never meeting the love of my life.

TreeTalk

I am ambulanced. I am humidified.

Humbled, the bodies tumbling. I sit

& stand corrected. I am treed.

Ariel Gordon

People are bashful. People eye the tree, the street, their
friends. They think
about what to say. CONFESS!

> I've been waiting for years for someone
> to poet-tree.
>
> Live well
> #RawHealth

TreeTalk

How do you diarize a tree?
A day of rest. A workweek. A school night.
They're all the same to a tree.

The church bells pour over the treetops
like maple syrup. Chimes & chimes. Peals.
The crows heaved into the air.

> "Little towns that worship big elms." — *Donald Culross Peattie*

Ariel Gordon

A Filipino girl writes *Peace and Serenity*
then runs for the bus, her lip quivering.

A small black beetle. Something green & fleeting
lands on the lens of my glasses. A leaf falls.

> "Leaves dark green and slightly rough above,
> paler green below, with soft hairs; edges double-
> toothed; leaf base not symmetrical; leaf veins
> prominent." — *Plants of the Western Boreal Forest*

TreeTalk

What is there to say about a tree, besides distance & time? Thick bark & waxy new leaves. The length of an afternoon, the spread of a century.

>Been living on this block for years. This tree is forever.

Ariel Gordon

I'm as slow as sap, mid-summer.

I'm as still as a leaf in the breeze: fixed

but vibrating. I oscillate like a fan.

TreeTalk

Run run run, a mother implores, chasing the bus, both hands full: a toddler's slow fingers & a full cup of juice. The afternoon sloshes. The bus driver waits until they've settled in before drifting forward…

Ariel Gordon

What spirit is in the tree?
Tired dryad is a traffic cop, an asphalt
gargoyle.

People tie drawings to the tree. Tie ideas & images.
People append. CONFESS!

> I've heard it said that trees move through time
> rather than space, as we do.

TreeTalk

I am shifting like a big-headed sunflower

but away from the sun. I am shrinking

like a violet.

Ariel Gordon

An older Indigenous man walks back
& forth under the tree,
his hair slicked back from his forehead.
His face gleams in the heat.
His shirt open, his nipples erect.

Cracked flagstones. Buckled pavement.
Wounds, the bark split & healed around them.
Chunks of bark on the sidewalk.

TreeTalk

> "You have to think of trees as infrastructure, and as infrastructure, they're the only one that actually accrues value with time." — *Martha Barwinsky*, city forester, as quoted in the *Winnipeg Free Press*.

Patioed. Parking-metered.
Bus-stopped. Stop-signed. Take-outed. Intersectioned.

I tell people: lean back. Rest your eyes in the canopy.
Put your fingers in the bark's fissures. CONFESS!

> "A big old specimen will have about 1 million leaves or an acre of leaf surface, and will cast a pool of shade 100 feet in diameter." — *Donald Culross Peattie*

Ariel Gordon

How do you know a tree?
You are three times as tall as me, double my age.
I can't help but maybe I won't hurt, this paper, this string.

SECRET: I used to think that there was such a thing as an acorn tree. Until I was 27.

TreeTalk

The breeze filters through.
Billows of talk, the passage of cars.
The leaves. The leaves, arrayed…

> "Elm leaves decompose rapidly, and are high in potassium and calcium, making American Elm a 'soil-improving' species." — *Plants of the Western Boreal Forest*

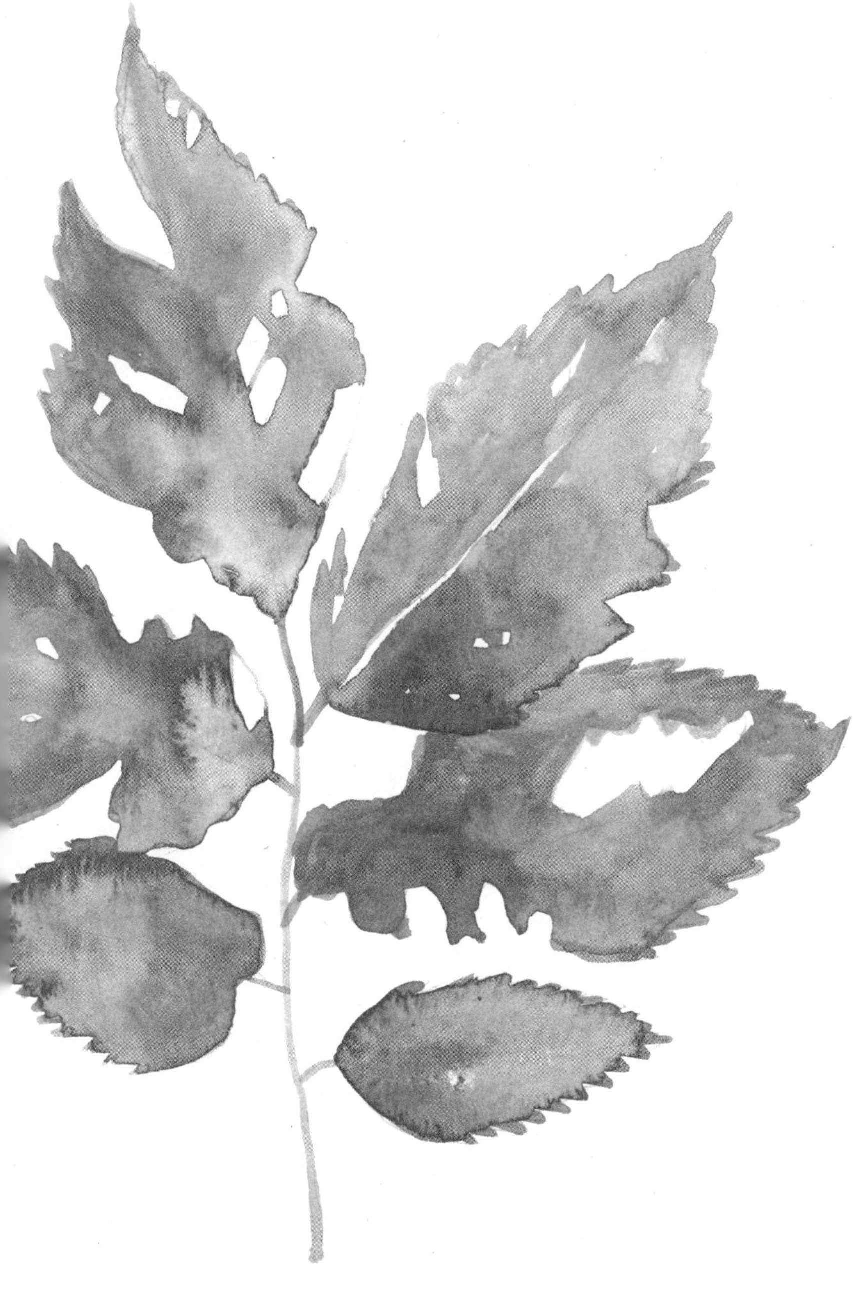

TreeTalk

His shirt open, a scar stands out on his belly,
showing the trajectory of a blade
as he bends to write: *This bird can sing.*

Open. Open. The sky grey, the humidity high. Garage
sales down side streets. Vines climbing brickwork.
Brown sparrows & orange lights.

Ariel Gordon

I can't stop staring at the extension cord, up in a branch.
The tree wired. In a few hours,
those lights will come on like fireflies, like stars.

SECRET: I'm scared of falling back into
old habits.

TreeTalk

An assembly of middle-aged trees, a chorus.
Taking a stand. Roots infiltrating below,
branches reaching above.
Filling the sky. Leafing out.

> "Is an elm tree a hardwood or softwood? Do elm
> trees grow fast? How long does an elm live for?"
> — *People Also Ask, Google.com*

Leaning towards the shade. The tree's wading pools
of coolness. Shallow relief.

Rain-dated. Sunday-ed.
Weather-delayed. Traffic-calmed.
Garage-sale-ed.

TreeTalk

The insistence of trees. Dying: branches falling
into traffic, leaves on windshields. Danger trees.
Widowmakers.

———

> We had a "Mom"
> who lived down the street,
> and she was so sweet
> We are here to remember her
> Her life was like this tree. (heart)
> 1921-2017

> "Elm wood is used for dry goods barrels, boxes,
> crates, furniture, flooring, panelling, caskets and
> boat-building." — *Plants of the Western Boreal
> Forest*

Ariel Gordon

The tree fills out. A fullness of words. A leafy manuscript. A streetwise folio.

    Carpe Tree-m—Seize the leaves.
    re-foliate—re-populate

    Veni vidi foliage.

TreeTalk

A man with a magnificent wolf's tail clipped to his belt. A streak of dyed hair gleams as he disappears down the street, sunglasses mirroring his eyes.

Ariel Gordon

I am sessile. Sidewalked. Sidelined.

So I make lists. A hierarchy of needs.

A laundry list of complaints.

After all, I'm attempting a canopy of poems.

TreeTalk

A brace of motorcycles. Dropped cutlery. The rattle
of leaves. Coughing. A girl who laughs
& laughs.

> You wear a macramé belt of poems you are
> powerless to remove or read.

Poems are edited by writers like me,
But only arborists can prune a tree.

Ariel Gordon

Clean living, dirty streets.
Elms are organic, self-cleaning, grounded.
Except we force-feed them pollution.
DED. Bulldozers.

In a furrow of shade, a fold of shadow, the day dimmed.

> "Crown umbrella-like on mature trees."
> — *Plants of the Western Boreal Forest*

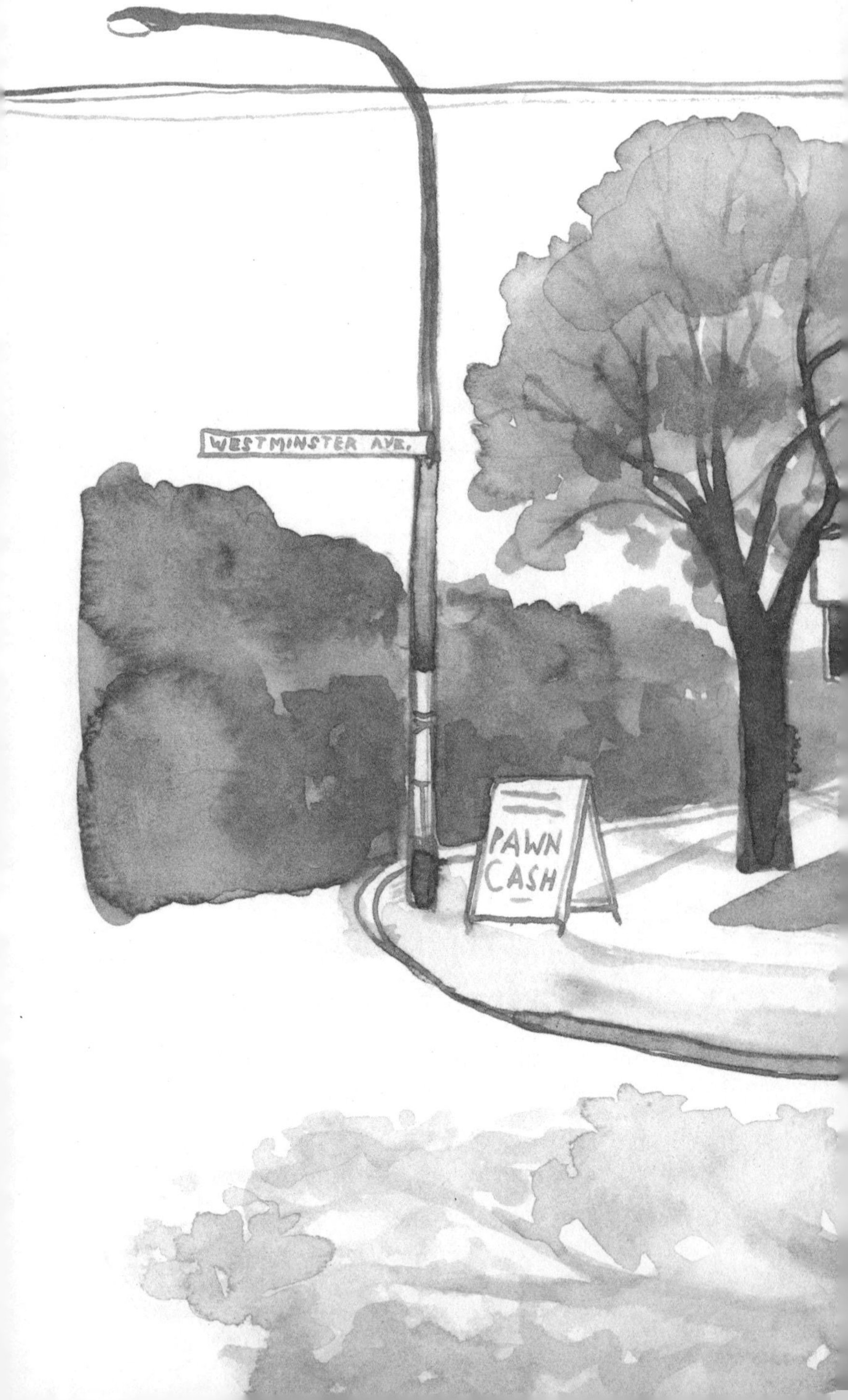
WESTMINSTER AVE.
PAWN
CASH

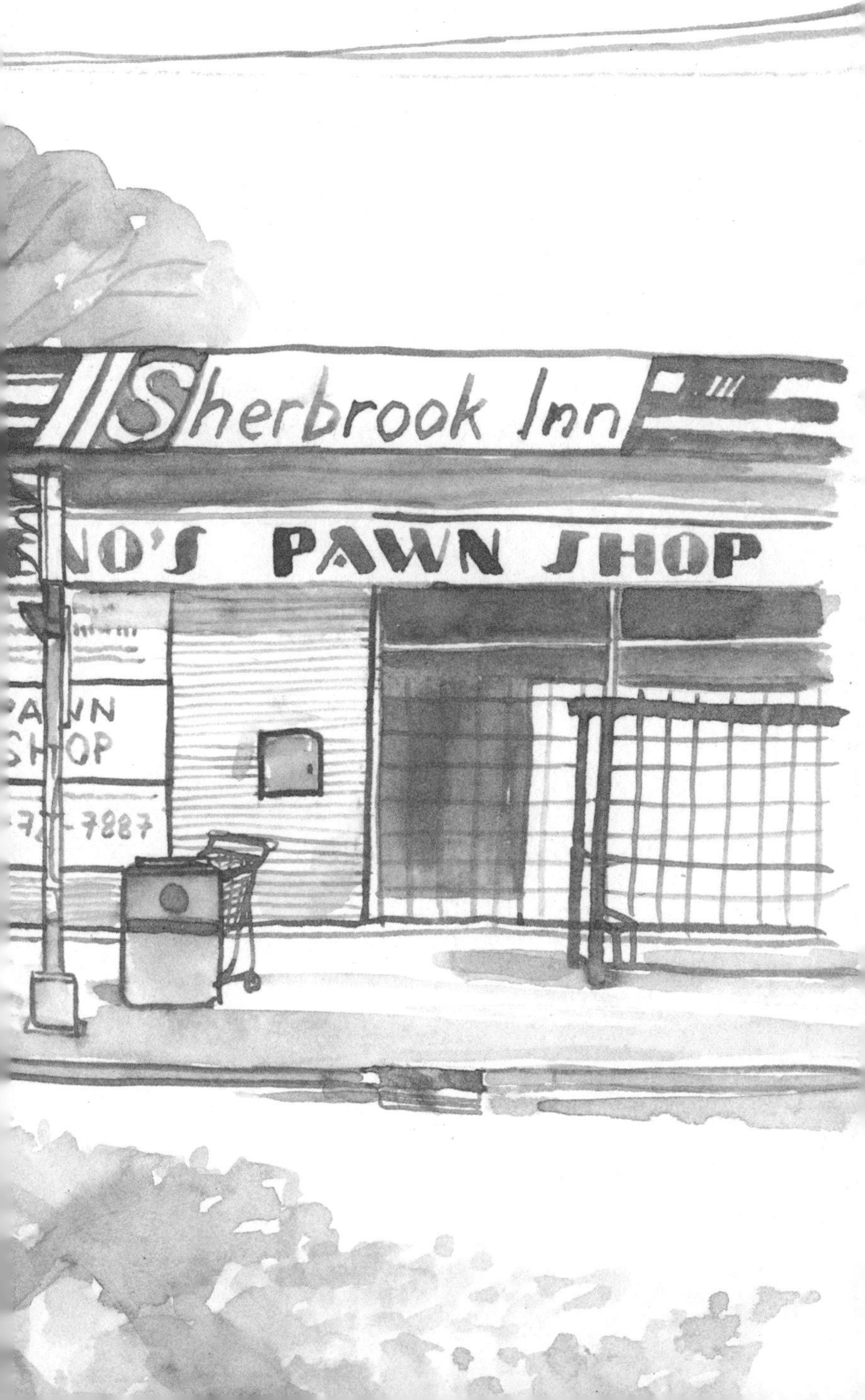
Sherbrook Inn
NO'S PAWN SHOP

TreeTalk

The waitress comes out to the patio to read the leaves, her arms suddenly empty of eggs & toast, chicken & waffles. Orders pour in; her hands open, her hands close.

Greening. Balding.
Buried. Leafed out.
Broken. Blooming.

> "We may never see trees of this size in Winnipeg again. " — *Martha Barwinsky, city forester, as quoted in the Winnipeg Free Press.*

Ariel Gordon

Wet currents all along an afternoon.
Umbrella-ed? More like soaked to the skin.
Porous. The temperature drops like a tree.

SECRET: I always have conflicting thoughts
and emotions.

TreeTalk

I am uninspired.

I am heavy, sodden.

I list.

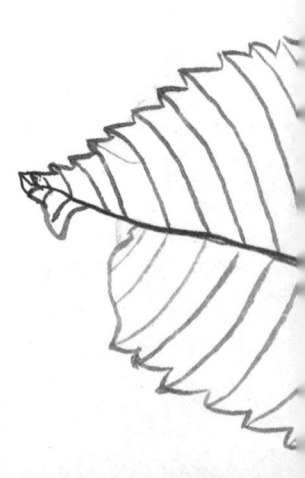

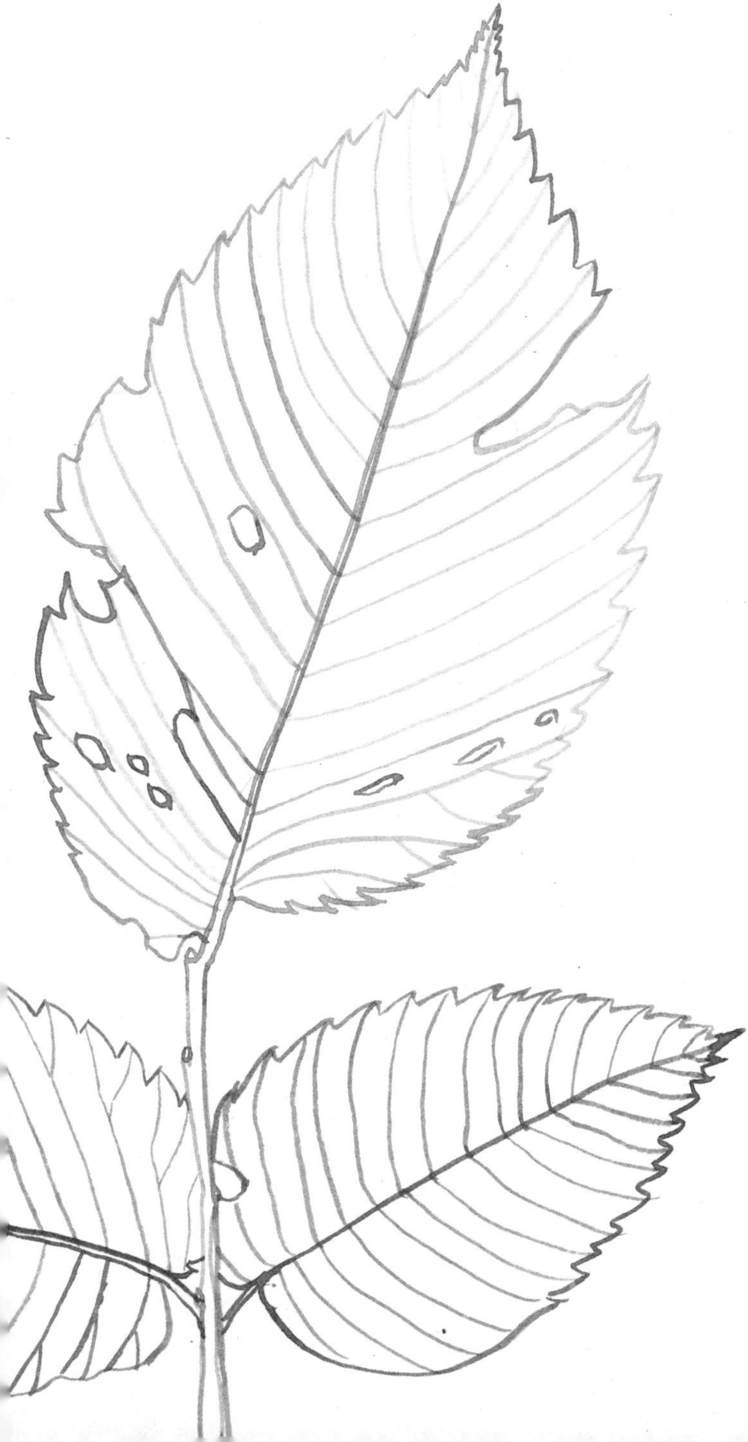

TreeTalk

Dear Tree, beautiful tree:
We sit here thinking about all that you have seen on this corner over the last 100 years. Thank you for standing strong. — *Jane + Matt*

The sky lurches, sweeps sideways, grey to one side, blue to the other. The heat waits. Moisture billows.
Another bus.

Ariel Gordon

Plantae
Angiosperms
Eudicots
Rosids
Rosales
Ulmaceae
Ulmus

TreeTalk

I am landscaped. Reupholstered

with a lattice of twigs, a mat

of leaves. I am treed but I need

to be pruned back.

Ariel Gordon

It starts to rain. Leaves shed water.
My poems get pulpy, bleed
ink & dye.

> Just because it is raining, it does not mean that
> you will never see the sun again.

The day is pendulous. Feet approach, depart.
Errands are run like dogs on a leash. Hours
on a patio somewhere.

TreeTalk

The last snippet of the day. I am undone. The string loosens.

The sun will rise, and I will try again. (drawing of a sun rising behind mountains + three clouds)

Ariel Gordon

Sun., 7/30, Hi/Lo: 32°C / 21°C

Garage sale sign appears overnight, taped to the tree.
A MILLION slightly used leaves for sale!

> Hobbits + trees are all you need!

> Peace and stuff!

The street quiets. Patio-talk. The creak of doors.
The sun moving across the table. A coffee here, a loaf
of bread there.

TreeTalk

I'm too hungover to write anything.

An old man with a sky-blue basketball jersey above & bright white knee socks below, his knees knobby, his skin the colour of a melted candle, waits at the bus stop.

Ariel Gordon

People pour secrets into the tree. Images.
Ideas. Penetrate the bark like beetles & feed.

> "If you want to be remembered for something you do, you will be well advised to do it under an elm—a great elm, for such a tree outlives the generations of men." — *Donald Culross Peattie*

Half-dead. Wilting. Flagging. Falling.
Stumped. Stilted. Listing.

TreeTalk

Across the street, a man with a bare chest, white & hairy with a red face, flexes his muscles, like he's a Sunday strongman. He turns slowly, like he's on a cake, preening in the window.

> "Twigs markedly zigzag, greyish brown, slightly hairy or hairless, often drooping." — *Plants of the Western Boreal Forest*

> You must think we two-leggeds make some odd choices with our freedom to move.

The pale man stares out at the strongman. He barely moves in his lukewarm bathtub of shade. The afternoon is indifferent, but the patio-dwellers giggle.

Ariel Gordon

Taking a break inside. The tree
retreats, the sun stays where it is. My head
buzzes like fluorescent lighting, like a handful of moths,
batting at a porch light.

A rattling skateboard. A suitcase.
A fast walker, all in black. Crows.

People, if anyone can keep a secret, it's a tree. Because
trees don't talk back. CONFESS!

TreeTalk

Not all leaves flutter, you know…

scraggly wolseley tree, trying not to be naked on the slowly gentrifying street, how many drunks have you seen marching down sherbrook in your lifetime?

Lights hung in the trees. Wires. Nests.
Garbage bags, shredded by updrafts. Homemade kites.

Every word ever muttered under its leaves,

every breath.

Ariel Gordon

I am in leaf. I am sugaring.

My skin itchy with sun, my fingers curled

around a pencil. I have learned how to breathe exhaust.

I am a filter feeder.

TreeTalk

"Indigenous to the province, it withstands the extremes of prairie winters, tolerates salt dumped on our streets, tolerates soil compaction and the vagaries of city works and operations departments." — *Trees Winnipeg*

How do you understand street trees?
First thing: they're not nestled in the forest. Not swaying

alongside a sibling.

Not nursed.

Ariel Gordon

Sitting on the patio, knees touching. Bareboned.
A tree instead of an awning.

> Thank you, protector. Thank you for holding
> light, shelter and keeping the whispers of our
> people as we pass you by, day by day.

A pair of miniature Dobermans decide to pick
a fight with a dog across the street.
The owner hauls them back.
A white girl brings her new hula-hoop to breakfast.
Floral dresses move like flowerbeds in the breeze.

TreeTalk

I am making an entire wedding's worth of confetti

but very, very slowly. I am making

industrial elm seed: SUPER samaras!

Ariel Gordon

Debarked. Unearthed. Canopied.
Out of your tree? Tree-shrugger.

> Tree of light + life—
> thank you for your quiet strength, and breath.
> (heart)

The lights change. The light swerves around corners, spills
over tables. The light. The light. Dappled.
Glaring. High noon.

TreeTalk

I'm heat-stroked. Iced.

I want the tree to move or talk.

I want a Slurpee.

Ariel Gordon

> "Why do you fight to save the elms? Why
> bother? They are all going to die anyway."
> — *Trees Winnipeg FAQ*

The utility of trees. Wearing thick layers of gig posters
& rusty staples. Bike locks, looped
around & secured. Garlanded with Xmas lights.

Poems are blades for fools like me,
But an axe is good enough for a tree.

TreeTalk

CONFESSION: When they resurfaced my street, weeks of machines, of rubble & rolls of fresh sod, I didn't defend my tree. I was resigned as its roots were scraped up, sliced off.

SECRET: The education system is a mess. Not just because of the conservative government, but because teachers who don't actually care about kids will not retire. They keep cashing a cheque while young, new teachers can't get jobs. The worst thing is we teachers aren't allowed to criticize the system for fear of reprimand. Why do you think I'm writing this anonymously for an art installation!?!?

Ariel Gordon

I feel like a reheated casserole. Like wood

that just won't light. I know there's no relief

for either of us. Another hot day.

TreeTalk

Birds build nests built of clothes hangers & shopping bags.
Nests of hair. Birds build in trees & eaves
& doorways.

Taking a break. What if the tree can see
what I'm thinking, that I'm not inspired anymore.
What if it's offended?

    Don't take leaf of your senses.

    YOU MAY BE RELAXING IN THE SHADE,
    BUT THESE LEAVES ARE WORKIN'!!

Ariel Gordon

The waitress stares across the street, murmurs: *Look at her legs – ah! Those blue shoes! That dress – ah! Should I yell?*

A person will walk 300 miles to reach another person. A tree will wait 300 years for a person to come to her.

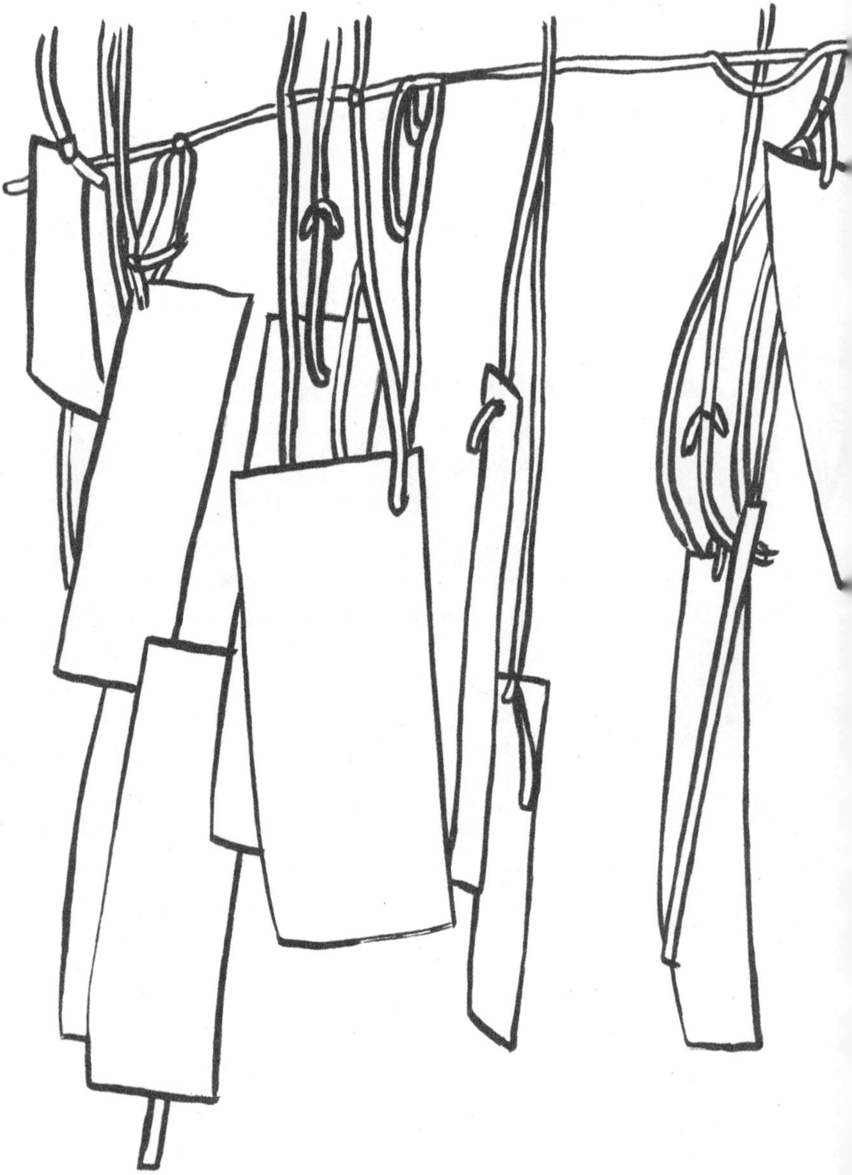

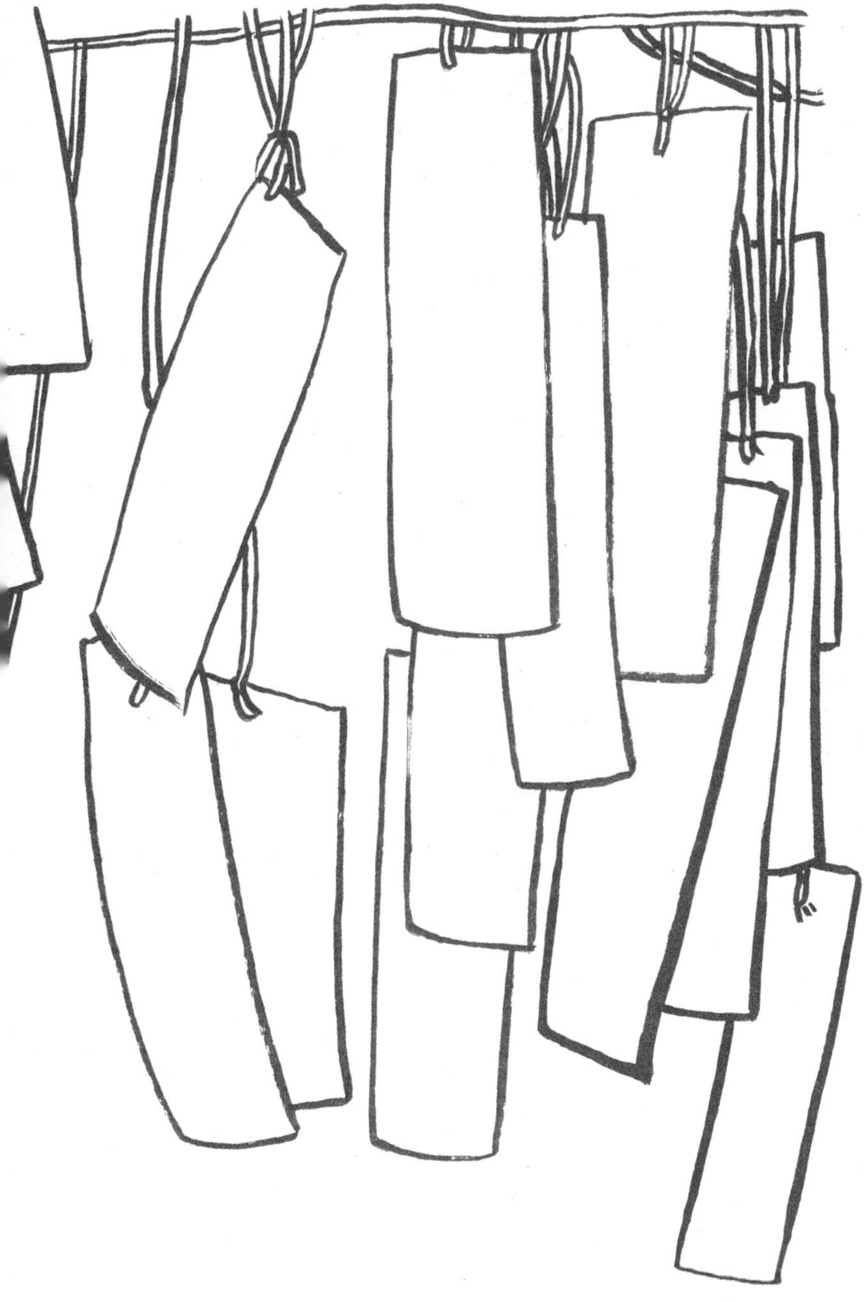

TreeTalk

Fourteen hours in, the tree is tinselled with my poems.
I'm humid, in & out. Exhaust
sticky on my skin. Dandelion fluff in my hair.

    It's not the tree's fault.

The poems move. People look up.
Poems as poison ivy, coated & waxy.
Poetry as invasive species.

Ariel Gordon

I am treed, but I am thinking of the coolness

of my bed, the sheets, the shade. I am convinced

my legs are sandbags leftover from the last flood.

TreeTalk

The tree spotlit. The tree golden-houred.
Sun on the pavement. Sun
on my table. It's time.

    Live Long and Prosper.

How do you leave a tree?
Should I pour my glass of lemon water

over your roots? Should I come back at midnight

& prune you?

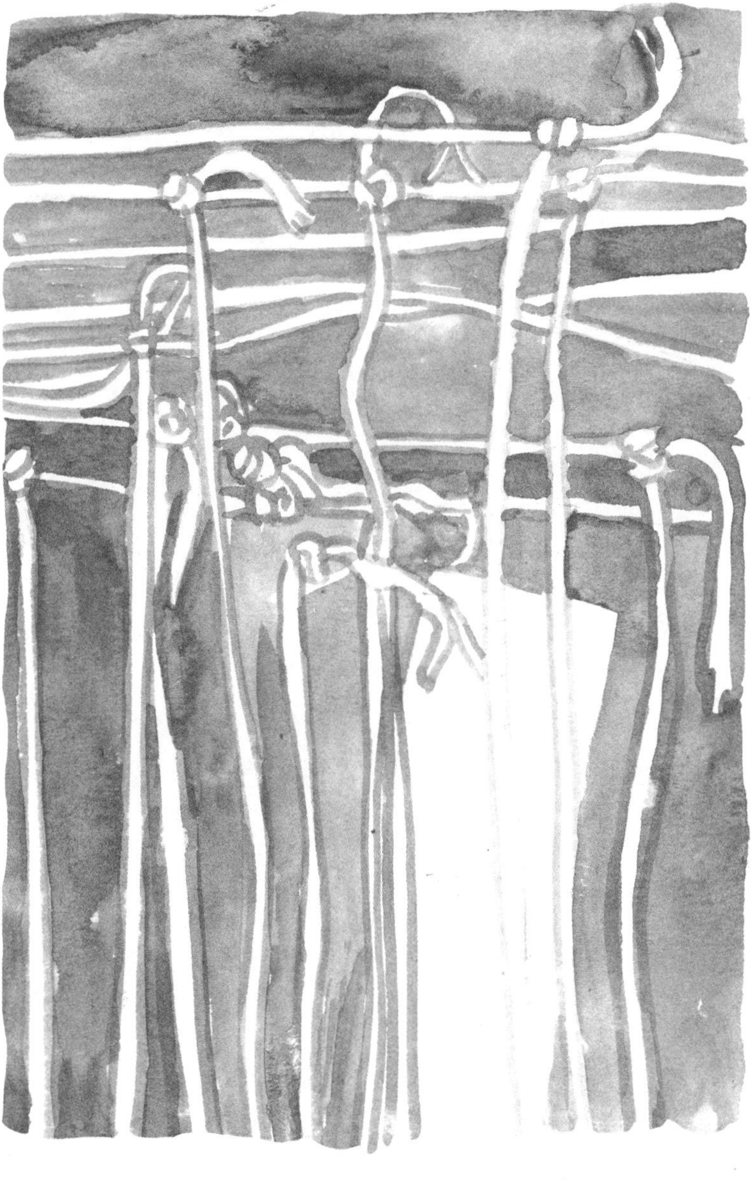

Appendix

In June 2017, just before my Synonym Art Consultation residency, Winnipeg's street trees were hosts for three infestations: cankerworm, elm spanworm and tent caterpillars.

This meant any number of worms dangling from trees on silky lines. Almost completely covering the sides of buildings. Colonizing the sidewalk.

Some people called it The Year of the Caterpillar. Other people dubbed it "Wormmageddon".

During this period, Winnipeggers wore worms on their shoulders and in their hair. They got worms in their mouths while biking.

When it wasn't worms, it was the loose strands of silk sticking to people's arms, legs and face anytime they were outside.

When it wasn't worms, it was the enormous quantities of worm poop raining down from the canopy, covering stairs and cars. And when it rained, you slipped around on a layer of liquefied worm poop.

But all of that was only an inconvenience. To the trees, the worms constituted a health hazard.

The worst-hit trees had their leaves eaten down to the stem, which means they spent the last few weeks of June growing a new canopy's worth of leaves.

In particular, this defoliation can make elm trees more susceptible to Dutch Elm Disease, because growing a new set of leaves uses up energy they'd otherwise use to combat infections.

The mature elm outside The Tallest Poppy is middle-aged, anywhere from 70 to 100 years old. It's survived round after round of construction, billows of pollution, drought, and even gig posters stapled to it. It didn't lose all its leaves to the worms but neither did it look like it was flourishing.

Part of the point of TreeTalk is that I was adding a new layer of leaves to the tree, replacing those munched up by the worms.

Part of the point was adding a new layer of ideas to our ideas on street trees.

Acknowledgments

Thanks to ArtsJunktion MB for the supplies that made this project possible: old green hanging folders, a ball of beige yarn, and an unused mop head.

Thanks to the Tallest Poppy generally for supporting SAC residencies and for the chicken-and-waffles and kale breakfasts that sustained me over the weekend. To TP chef-owner Talia Syrie, in particular, who brought me a JUMBO Piña Colada Freezie when I was starting to feel like a melted candle.

Thanks to Andrew Eastman and Chloe Chafe at Synonym Art Consultation for all their work and for being so great to work with.

Thanks to photographer Mike Deal for the documentation & to the *Winnipeg Free Press*' Scott Gibbons for publishing an early/much shorter version of this poem.

I took TreeTalk to Sage Hill's 2018 Spring Poetry Colloquium. After an overcommitted spring, I had the time and space to transcribe all 234 poems, print them out, and then make with the scissors. I spent the next two days arranging and rearranging, taping finished sections to the wall.

My evergreen thanks to Yvonne Blomer, who I trust to look at drafts, who I rely on for most things in this writing life. I am also enormously grateful to Lisa Pasold, who walked under the trees of the poem and reported back....

Finally, thanks to Matt from At Bay Press for waggling his eyebrows & asking for a poem.

I am also glad that my stepsister/visual-artist Natalie Baird came and had breakfast at The Tallest Poppy with her friends, contributing two drawings to the tree. When Matt approached me about doing a book together, I knew from his previous titles that he would be amenable to my including some of Natalie's artworks. I'd been waiting YEARS for the chance to work with her....

Photograph by Mikaela MacKenzie

Natalie Baird is a visual artist, filmmaker, and community-based researcher based in Winnipeg, Manitoba. Natalie completed a bachelor of environmental science from the University of Manitoba in 2014, where she explored film-making as a tool for environmental action. Her documentary, animation, and video-installation work has been screened and exhibited across Canada. She has an embedded community practice, working as an arts facilitator and artist-in-residence in drop-in art centres and personal care homes. In 2016 Natalie returned to the University of Manitoba for a master of environment, leading arts-based research projects about the social dimensions of climate change in Nunavut.

Photograph by Mike Deal

Ariel Gordon is the Winnipeg-based author of two collections of urban-nature poetry with Windsor's Palimpsest Press, both of which won the Lansdowne Prize for Poetry. She is the co-editor, with Tanis MacDonald and Rosanna Deerchild, of the anthology *GUSH: menstrual manifestos for our times* (Frontenac House, 2018). Ariel just completed the 5th anniversary edition of Writes of Spring, a National Poetry Month project that's published in the *Winnipeg Free Press* in partnership with the Winnipeg International Writers Festival. Her most recent book, a collection of essays called *Treed: Walking in Canada's Urban Forest* (Wolsak & Wynn, 2019), was shortlisted for the Carol Shields Winnipeg Book Award at the Manitoba Book Awards and received an honourable mention for ALECC's 2020 Alanna Bondar Memorial Book Prize for the Environmental Humanities and Creative Writing.